D1060588

ON THE HARDWOOD

ZACH WYNER

On the Hardwood: Indiana Pacers

MVP Books
2255 Calle Clara
La Jolla, CA 92037

MVP Books is an imprint of Book Buddy Digital Media, Inc., 42982 Osgood Road, Fremont, CA 94539

MVP Books publications may be purchased for
educational, business, or sales promotional use.

Cover and layout design by Jana Ramsay
Copyedited by Susan Sylvia
Photos by Getty Images

ISBN: 978-1-61570-852-9 (Library Binding)
ISBN: 978-1-61570-836-9 (Soft Cover)

TABLE OF CONTENTS

Chapter 1

BASKETBALL'S BIRTHPLACE

NBA

Synonymous means: closely associated with or suggestive of something. For even the most casual hoops fan, the state of Indiana is synonymous with one thing: basketball. This is just as true today as it was in 1925 when the creator of basketball, James Naismith, wrote, "Basketball really had its origin in Indiana, which remains the center of the sport." For nearly a century, Indiana has been hoops obsessed. From its smallest high school gymnasiums to Branch McCracken court, home of the legendary Hoosiers of Indiana University, basketball has captured the imagination of the people.

For many residents of the state, it's the quality of Indiana

basketball that is their greatest source of pride. Indiana natives can lay claim to producing the greatest high school basketball tournament

The inventor of basketball, Dr. James Naismith.

in the country, as well as two of the greatest players in the history of the NBA, Larry Bird and Oscar Robertson. In October of 2012, the Indiana Fever and their star player Tamika Catchings brought home their first WNBA title. In addition to these badges of honor, the state is home to one of the country's most beloved professional sports franchises: the Indiana Pacers.

Placing a professional basketball team in Indiana seemed like a no-brainer. Since the 1920s, fans had come out in droves to see the sport played at an amateur level. But if a professional team wanted to develop a loyal following, they would have to tap into the pride that residents took in the quality of basketball played by boys and girls from the state's tiniest farm towns to its largest metropolises. Of course, there was one quick

Tamika Catchings of the Indiana Fever shoots over an opposing player during the 2012 WNBA Finals.

and efficient way to reach this goal: win championships.

The Indiana Pacers were founded in 1967 when they joined the American Basketball Association (ABA). Coached by Bob "Slick" Leonard, the Pacers advanced to five finals in nine years. Because of star players like Mel Daniels and Roger Brown, the Pacers won the ABA title in 1970. Then, following the 1970-71 season, Daniels and Brown were joined by one of Indiana's greatest homegrown talents, George McGinnis. Born in Indianapolis, Indiana, the muscular 6'8" 235-pound McGinnis starred as both a high school player and then at the collegiate level at Indiana University.

Mel Daniels shoots a hook shot over ABA legend and NBA Hall of Famer Artis Gilmore.

After leading the Big Ten in scoring in 1971 at 30 points per game, McGinnis was drafted into the ABA.

"The Rajah"

In 1997, Roger Brown was one of seven players selected to the ABA All-Time Team.

Frontcourt Dominance

Mel Daniels earned ABA MVP honors in 1969 and 1971 and was the ABA's all-time leader in rebounding with 15 per game.

He joined the already outstanding Pacers for the 1971-72 season and the team became an absolute force, winning the next two ABA titles.

By winning three championships in four years, the Pacers attracted thousands of devoted fans and established themselves as an ABA dynasty.

When the ABA merged with the NBA in 1976, Pacers fans hoped that the winning would continue. The Pacers had been one of the premier ABA franchises. In exhibition games before the 1976 season, ABA teams had performed quite well against the NBA's best. But the Pacers had a major hurdle to overcome, an obstacle that had nothing to do with talent. While it was true

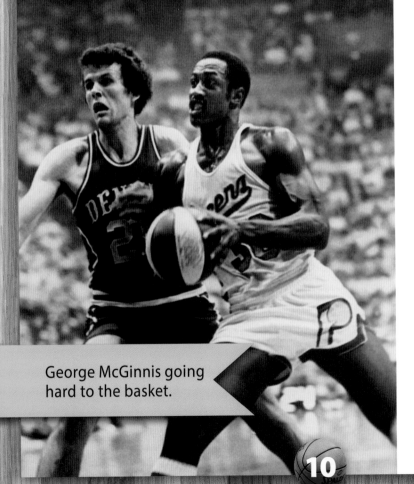

George McGinnis going hard to the basket.

that the team had enjoyed great success in the late 1960s and early 1970s, the Pacers entered the NBA as one of its poorest franchises.

Conditions of the ABA/NBA merger stated that ABA teams must pay a $3.2 million fee to join the league as well as financially compensate the ABA teams that had not been invited to join. In addition, another harsh term of the merger said that none of the former ABA teams would receive money generated by national television broadcasts for their first four years. These factors meant deep financial trouble for the Pacers.

In order to stay afloat, the Pacers sold off most of their talent. As a result, their first year in the NBA was not a successful one. They finished

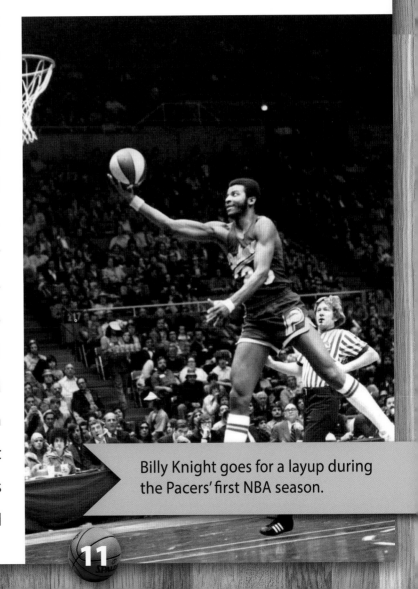

Billy Knight goes for a layup during the Pacers' first NBA season.

11

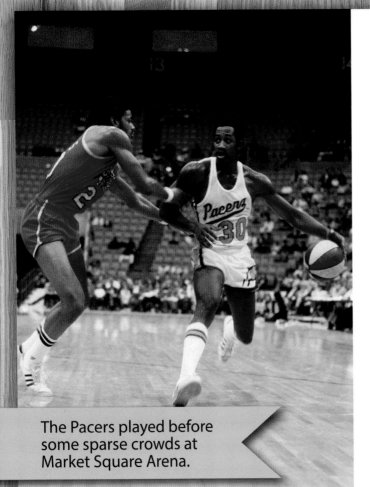

The Pacers played before some sparse crowds at Market Square Arena.

dwindled. By the time the 1977 season rolled around, it looked as though the team's days might be numbered.

Without any of the big TV money that helped NBA teams survive, the Pacers could not simply rely on tickets purchased at the arena on the night of the game. They needed to sell season tickets in order to pay their players and team employees. They needed fans to lend their support before the season started, to show that they were behind their team whether or not their team won a lot of games that year. Pacers ownership announced to the media that unless season-ticket sales reached 8,000 by the end of July, the club would be

the season in fifth place in the Midwest division with a record of 36 wins and 46 losses. Ticket sales

Cream of the Crop

The Pacers were one of four teams to join the NBA. The other three were the New York Nets, San Antonio Spurs, and Denver Nuggets.

sold and likely moved.

In response to this public call for support, WTTV, the local television station that carried Pacers' games, held a 24-hour telethon to keep the team in Indiana. For 23 hours and 50 minutes, players and coaches waited for their fate to be determined while operators took ticket orders from loyal fans. Ten minutes before the show was set to go off the air, it was announced that team officials had reached the 8,000-ticket goal. The state of Indiana had saved their team. They

had given the Pacers a chance to rediscover the greatness they had achieved in the ABA.

Bob "Slick" Leonard coaching the Pacers up during a timeout.

Chapter 2
A HISTORY OF EXCELLENCE

The social landscape of Indiana is not what it once was. Larger cities and larger suburban areas surrounding those cities have led to larger schools. The single-class basketball tournament, where all high schools no matter their size competed for the state title, was dropped in 1997. But changes in the size of schools and the overall population do not diminish the story of the 1954 Milan High School Indians. Immortalized in the classic sports film "Hoosiers," the story of Milan High will forever be a part of American sports lore and a lasting example of the value of teamwork.

In 1954, Milan, Indiana was a small town with a total population of about 1,150 people. The enrollment at Milan High School

David vs. Goliath

Muncie Central's home gymnasium held 7,600 people, about 6,500 more than the entire population of Milan.

was 161 students. In most parts of the world, a smaller pool to draw from means fewer gifted athletes. This is what is sometimes referred to as "the law of averages." The law of averages dictates that a school with 3,000 students will have more talented athletes than a school with less than 200. However, in Milan, the law of averages did not apply. Led by Bobby Plump, a 6'1" guard with a sweet shooting touch, the Indians competed with and beat teams from larger cities all season long. Then, in the single-class tournament that followed the regular season, they did what no team from a school their size ever did again—they won the state title. In the state final, Milan High beat the hugely favored, eight-time state champion Muncie Central Bearcats, 32-30.

On their way to greatness, the Milan Indians also beat Crispus Attucks High School and their star, future NBA Hall of Famer Oscar Robertson. Of course, Oscar was only a sophomore that year. And it was what he accomplished in his junior and senior seasons at Crispus Attucks that made him a national figure. In 1954, Crispus Attucks fell short of their goal, losing to the historic Milan Indians and failing to make it to the state finals. However, in the coming years, they made some history of their own. In 1955 Crispus Attucks became the first all-black school to win a state high school championship. In 1956, they won it again.

Founded in 1927, Crispus Attucks High had been created as a school solely for African-American students. No one ever wants to be told where he or she can or can't go to school. But for many black students, leaving an all-white school to attend Crispus Attucks meant a better education. You see, at that time in the United States, African American teachers were allowed to attend universities but not teach there. Because of this, every teacher at Crispus Attucks had a Master's degree or a Ph. D.

Impressive Alumni

Crispus Attucks graduates include US Representative Julia Carson, writer Janet Langhart-Cohen, and legendary jazz musicians Wes Montgomery, Freddie Hubbard, James Spaulding and J. J. Johnson.

Crispus Attucks High School had more than an outstanding basketball team; it had some of the best-educated students in the country. Oscar Robertson and Crispus Attucks did more than just dominate the competition—they raised national awareness and helped promote equality.

Making history is something with which the legendary Hoosiers of Indiana University are well acquainted. The Hoosiers' five NCAA Championships (1940, 1953, 1976, 1981, and 1987) ties them for third all-time with the University of North Carolina. Every four-year Hoosier since 1973 has made the NCAA tournament, and every four-year player since 1950

Oscar Robertson and teammates accept the Indiana High School Basketball Championship trophy.

has played for the Hoosiers while they were nationally ranked. In other words, a basketball player who puts on the famous red and white candy-striped warm-up pants of Indiana University does so with an awareness of history and a sense of pride.

Isaiah Thomas cuts down the nets at the 1981 Final Four after leading the Hoosiers to their fourth national championship.

the famed Hoosiers to the Final Four. For a precious few, that dream comes true. But with high honors come high expectations. Indiana fans expect a lot of their team. Players who wear the Hoosiers' red and white know this, and for some, the pressure of playing for Indiana University has been too much. For one such player, the path to greatness was through a quieter place; a place where he would be given space to grow at the small-town pace of his rural Indiana home.

Over the years, Hoosier fans have been privileged to watch the likes of George McGinnis, Quinn Buckner, Steve Alford, and the great Isaiah Thomas lead their team to glory. For generations, young boys and girls from Indiana and all across the country have dreamed of leading

Larry Bird was raised in French Lick, a small town in the southern part of Indiana. After being a highly recruited high school player, Bird attended Indiana University for 24 days before dropping out. The sheer size of the school had been too much. Bird returned to French Lick and took a job with the streets department. Unable to let go of the idea of going to college and playing basketball, Bird quit his job picking up trash and repairing roads to attend Indiana State University in nearby Terre Haute. It was at this small school, playing with a group of unknown players that Larry Bird became Larry Legend.

Before Larry Bird, the Indiana State Sycamores had never made the NCAA tournament. By March of

Larry Bird leads the Indiana State Sycamores against the Spartans of Michigan State.

1979, they entered the tournament with a record of 28 wins and zero losses. They were the only undefeated team in the nation. Bird had led the team in all major

Gym Rat
While attending Springs Valley High School in French Lick, Bird could be found shooting baskets in the gym before, between and after classes.

Unstoppable

After three seasons at Indiana State, Bird left as the fifth-highest scorer in NCAA history. He finished his collegiate career with an average of 30.3 points per game.

statistical categories, averaging 29 points, 15 rebounds, and six assists per game, and in the tournament, the Sycamores advanced all the way to the finals. There they encountered Magic Johnson's Michigan State Spartans. While the Sycamores were undefeated, many Indiana natives recognized the similarity to the 1954 state final between Milan High and Muncie Central. Besides Magic Johnson, Michigan State had a number of future NBA players on their roster. The Sycamores had a number of excellent team players who knew their roles, but Bird was the only one who would go on to succeed in the NBA.

On March 26th, 1979, Michigan State beat Indiana State 75-64 to capture the NCAA title. The game is still the most-watched broadcast in the history of college

Magic Johnson dunks over a Sycamore during the most watched game in college basketball history.

basketball. It would be the first of many epic clashes between Magic and Larry and the birth of arguably the greatest rivalry in the history of professional team sports. As members of the Los Angeles Lakers and Boston Celtics, Magic and Bird would cause an explosion of interest in the NBA that would forever change the game of basketball. But to Larry's hometown of French Lick, and countless other towns across the state of Indiana, the rest of the world was just playing catch-up. The love affair between Indiana and basketball was already decades old. While the rest of the nation celebrated the rebirth of the NBA, Indiana natives continued to wait patiently for a star to emerge and lead their hometown Pacers to glory.

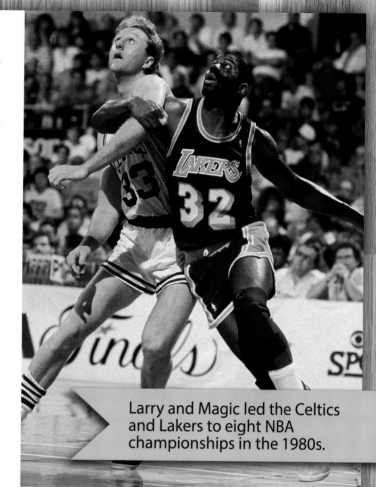

Larry and Magic led the Celtics and Lakers to eight NBA championships in the 1980s.

Vengeance Is Mine

Larry avenged his NCAA title loss to Magic by leading the Celtics over the Lakers for the NBA Championship in 1984.

Chapter 3
SHOOTERS DUEL

By 1991, Larry Bird's Boston Celtics were showing their age. During the 1980s, Bird had led the Celtics to three championships, won three MVP awards and cemented his legacy as the greatest small forward in the history of the game. While many remember him for his clutch shooting, it was as a passer that he surpassed every forward before him. Still, Bird's career shooting statistics couldn't be more impressive. Only six players in the history of the NBA have managed to shoot over 50 percent from the field, 40 percent from three-point range and 90 percent from the free throw line over the course of an entire season. Bird did it twice. In the 1991 playoffs, Larry Bird squared off against another sharpshooter, a young man who was soon to become the third member of the highly exclusive "50-40-90 Club." His name was Reggie Miller.

Finishing the regular season with a record of 41 wins and 41 losses, few people expected the 1991 Indiana Pacers to give the mighty Celtics much trouble. But those who had anticipated an easy win for the Celtics hadn't considered how many points the Pacers were able to score when they pushed the tempo. Over the previous two seasons, Reggie Miller had become the leading scorer of a core of young players that included Chuck Person, Detlef Schrempf, and the 7'4" center

of 50 (50%) from three-point range and score 48 points per game. Respected for his ability to hit shots from any distance, Person recalls the series this way: "We were young and inexperienced. Boston had great leaders in Larry, Robert, and Kevin. But we were young, fast, and brash." Person hit seven three-pointers in Game 2 at the Boston Garden and the fast and brash Pacers shocked the Celtics by taking the series to a winner-take-all Game 5. It was one for the ages.

Game 5 is best remembered for Larry Bird's remarkable play through pain—the Hall of Famer suffered a concussion when his head violently collided with the floor in the second quarter. Bird went to the locker room and stayed

known as the "Dunking Dutchman," Rik Smits. If there was one thing this core could do, it was score.

In their first-round series against the Celtics, Miller and Person combined to shoot an amazing 25

there. Many doubted whether he would return. However, during the third quarter, Bird emerged from the tunnels that led to the locker rooms and jogged to the Boston bench. The fans went absolutely wild. These days, if you ask an NBA fan to recall the rest of that game, many of them will remember Larry Bird playing through the pain. They will remember him sinking shots from all over the court and giving the Celtics a huge lead. Fewer fans remember that the young Pacers, unfazed by Bird's heroics and the exuberant Boston crowd, mounted a furious comeback and almost stole the series.

Oh-So Close
In Game 5, Chuck Person shot five of nine from three-point range and scored 32 points.

In the fourth quarter of that legendary Game 5, the Pacers cut a 112-96 deficit to two points. With seconds left, they had possession of the ball with a chance to win the game and shock the world. Sadly

Rick "The Dunking Dutchman" Smits attempts a shot over Hall of Fame center, Robert "Chief" Parish.

The young Pacers squad pulled together and almost shocked the world.

Miller would take the final shot of a close Pacers game.

After a disappointing 1991-92 season, the Pacers' general manager Donnie Walsh traded Person and began building the team around Reggie. Before the 1993-94 season, he also traded Detlef Schrempf for forward Derrick McKey. The trade was highly criticized, but McKey brought a defensive toughness that the Pacers had been lacking. By the time the team won their final eight games of the season and then won back-to-back playoff series against the Magic and the Hawks, the criticisms ceased. This Pacers squad was for real. Only one obstacle remained standing in

for Pacers fans, Chuck Person's 26-foot jumper missed its mark and the Celtics held on to win. Person had played an unbelievable series. No one could second-guess coach Bob Hill's decision to put the ball in his hands. But that day would be the last time for a long time that anyone with a name other than

the way of a trip to the NBA Finals: the New York Knicks.

In 1994 the New York Knicks were hungry. For years their star center, Patrick Ewing, had been losing out on chances to advance to the NBA Finals because of Michael Jordan's Chicago Bulls. But in 1993, Michael had gone into an early retirement in order to pursue his dreams of playing professional baseball. The Eastern Conference crown was suddenly there for the taking. Facing an inexperienced Pacers squad in the Eastern Conference Finals, the Knicks were confident that this was their year. Despite his numbers, few people outside of

Indiana realized the big-game player that Reggie had become. Few suspected that he would soon be a household name, a player

During the 1993-94 season, Ewing was in his prime, averaging 25 points, 11 rebounds and three blocks per game.

Reggie shoots a three-pointer over John Starks during the 1994 playoffs.

regarded as one of the greatest clutch shooters in the history of the game.

Some players are remembered for what they accomplish over the course of an entire career— for how many points they average in a season or how many rebounds they grab. Others are remembered for their style— for the way they dunk the ball, cross over a defender, or throw a behind-the-back pass. Some players are remembered for winning championships, for being at the top of the sport year after year. Others are remembered for individual games, for performing at the highest possible level when everything is on the line. Reggie Miller is one of those players. Game

5 of the 1994 Eastern Conference playoffs was one of those games.

Early in the fourth quarter of Game 5, playing in front of a hostile New York crowd, the Pacers trailed the Knicks by 15 points. To add insult to injury, the great American filmmaker and avid Knicks fan, Spike Lee, was taunting Reggie from his front row seat. To all who were watching, it looked like the game was over. Then like a bolt of lightning, Reggie Miller struck. He torched the Knicks defense, hitting five of five threes and scoring 25 fourth-quarter points. The dumbstruck crowd watched helplessly as Reggie jawed with Spike Lee and the Pacers stunned the Knicks, 93-86.

The New York Knicks would bounce back to beat the Pacers in seven games, but not before a superstar and a fierce rivalry had been born. Countless Indiana boys and girls grow up dreaming of playing basketball for the Indiana Hoosiers. But before Reggie, few had the audacity to dream of single-handedly dismantling the Knicks in a playoff game at Madison Square Garden. Reggie's play inspired young fans to dream of winning the biggest games on the biggest stages. And it wouldn't be the last time. The battle between Reggie and the Knicks was far from over.

All The World's A Stage
Following the 1994 playoffs, Reggie was selected to be a member of the U.S. National Team and led them to a gold medal at the World Basketball Championships in Toronto.

Chapter 4
BETTING ON THE BRUIN

When Pacers General Manager Donnie Walsh first witnessed Reggie playing for the UCLA Bruins, he saw a player with exceptional basketball intelligence and scoring ability. In other words, he saw the potential for greatness. But great players are not born great. Great players become great through hard work and a single-minded devotion to the game of basketball. They are driven by their desire to win, to be the best player on the court. In the case of Reggie Miller, he was driven by the desire to be the best in his driveway.

Reggie Miller was born and raised in Riverside, California, thousands of miles from Indiana and the rural landscape that nurtured Larry Bird. One of five

Running In The Family

Reggie's talented siblings include sister Cheryl (a Hall of Fame women's basketball player) and brother Darrell (former catcher for the California Angels).

children, Reggie grew up in an athletically gifted family. While he would grow into every bit the athlete that his brothers and sisters were, he would have to be patient. Born with a deformity in his hips, for the first

With the 11th overall pick in the 1987 Draft, Donnie Walsh selected Reggie Miller.

four years of his life, Reggie could not walk without the assistance of leg braces. Some doctors believed that he would never overcome the handicap. But when Reggie was five, the braces came off. He wasted no time in catching up to his gifted siblings.

Reggie is the younger brother of Cheryl Miller, former college basketball star and arguably the greatest women's basketball player who ever lived. It was his rivalry with his sister that drove Reggie to be the player he was.

One story the Millers are fond of telling is the time Reggie scored 40 points in a high school game. During the car ride home, Reggie bragged to his older sister (whose team had also had a game that day) about what a great game he'd had and how many points he'd scored. Cheryl congratulated her little brother but did not seem overly impressed. When he finally asked her how many she had scored, she smiled. "One hundred and five," she said. Reggie's jaw dropped. If he wanted to outdo his big sister, his work was far from done. By 1987,

Reggie sits with big sister Cheryl during a press conference prior to his number-retiring ceremony at Conseco Fieldhouse.

Reggie had worked hard enough to convince Pacers General Manager Donnie Walsh that he was worth the Pacers' first-round draft pick.

A former college basketball player at the University of North Carolina, Donnie Walsh knew a star when he saw one. In 1987, Walsh's belief in Reggie became a source of controversy, thrusting both men into the spotlight.

The general manager of a basketball team has many duties, but their primary job is to select team personnel. This means the signing, trading, and drafting of players. One of the greatest challenges about this job is that nearly every fan thinks that they know what's best for the team.

In 1987, fans felt what was best for the Pacers was to select hometown hero and Indiana Hoosiers star, Steve Alford. Donnie Walsh felt differently. Instead of selecting Alford, he made the highly unpopular decision to draft Reggie Miller, the lean and lanky shooter from UCLA. The outrage voiced by Pacers fans would quickly fade. Reggie developed into a Hall of Famer while Steve Alford never managed to adjust to the speed of the NBA game. Alford had been the safe bet. Had Walsh drafted him, no one would have complained when he didn't pan out. But the safe bet made no sense to Walsh if it meant passing on a star.

In 1995, the season after Reggie's breakout series against the Knicks, Donnie Walsh brought another

Floor general Mark Jackson calls out a play against the New York Knicks.

Basketball fans wanted to see him do the impossible again. They didn't have to wait long.

Game 1 of the Eastern Conference Semifinals was played in New York, on the same court where Reggie had dropped 25 in the fourth quarter a year before. By now, Knicks fans knew that when Reggie was on the court, no lead was safe. But even the most anxious New Yorkers had to feel pretty good with the Knicks leading by six points with 17 seconds left in the game. Then Reggie hit a deep three. That's okay, thought Knicks fans. We've still got a three-point lead and the ball. Then Reggie stole the inbounds pass, dribbled out beyond the three-point arc and Bang! He hit another three. The crowd watched

standout from the 1987 NBA Draft to Indiana: point guard Mark Jackson. Jackson brought stability and great passing to the Pacers' backcourt. And of course his favorite target was Reggie. That postseason, when Miller, Jackson, and the Pacers again squared off with the Knicks in the playoffs, fans were ready. Reggie and his flare for the dramatic weren't going to surprise anyone this time.

in horror as the Knicks missed two free throws and then fouled Reggie on the rebound, sending him to the free-throw line. Reggie sank the foul shots and with them, the Knicks' spirits. In a span of 8.9 seconds, he had scored eight points. The Pacers won the game, 107-105.

The Pacers would go on to beat the Knicks in seven games, but they were once again denied a trip to the NBA Finals. In the Eastern Conference Finals, they were defeated by Shaquille O'Neal's Orlando Magic.

Two seasons later, a change was made. In 1996, the Pacers had seen their playoff chances shattered when Reggie broke his eye socket. Then, in the 1996-97 season, they failed to make the playoffs for the first time in eight years. Coach Larry Brown

stepped aside and the greatest player in the history of the state of Indiana picked up the clipboard. Larry Legend had returned home to become a fixture of Indiana Pacers basketball. His job was to lead

Reggie launches a three against the Knicks at Madison Square Garden.

35

them where no coach had led them before: the NBA Finals.

In Larry Bird's first season at the helm, he coached the Pacers to a 58-24 record, the best in franchise history. Joining Miller, Smits, and Jackson on the court was five-time All-Star Chris Mullin. In Miller and Mullin, the Pacers now had two of the best three-point shooters in the history of the game. This time when the Pacers met the Knicks in the Eastern Conference Semifinals, it was no contest. The Pacers won the series in five games to return to the Eastern Conference Finals. Unfortunately for them, Michael Jordan's baseball career hadn't gone

Reggie and Michael take a moment to catch their breath.

as planned. In 1995, the superstar had returned to the NBA and by the spring of 1998, he was looking to lead the Bulls to a third consecutive NBA title. Bird, Miller, and the rest of the Pacers knew that this was the best Pacers team since the ABA days. They also knew that to get where they wanted to go, they'd have to beat the best basketball player of all time.

In the 1998 Eastern Conference Finals, the Pacers fought admirably. Reggie continued his playoff heroics. He scored 13 points in the final four-and-one-half minutes of Game 3 on a sprained ankle. Then in Game 4, he hit a three-pointer with 2.7 seconds on the clock to seal the victory. This was Reggie being Reggie, excelling on the stage that he had dreamed of his whole life: playing the best in the world for a chance at the NBA crown.

The Pacers took the Bulls to a seventh game. Looking back, players and fans can only shake their heads and wonder what might have been. Indiana outplayed the champs, shooting a better percentage from the field and holding a slim lead late into the fourth quarter. But a combination of poor free-throw shooting (the Pacers missed 14 from the line) and an inability to control the boards (they were out-rebounded by 18) doomed them. If only they had made their free

Rivalry Reborn

With All-Star center Patrick Ewing sidelined, the Knicks stunned the Pacers in the lockout-shortened 1999 playoffs and became the first #8 seed to make the NBA Finals.

Jalen Rose rises for the layup.

throws, if only that fourth quarter lead had been a bit larger, they would have likely held off the Bulls' final charge. Alas, the Pacers faded in the final two minutes and the Bulls won the game, 88-83.

After the 1998 season, Jordan walked away from the sport for the second time with six NBA titles and the unofficial title of world's greatest basketball player. The Eastern Conference was again up for grabs. In the 1999-2000 season, Reggie Miller and Indiana basketball fans finally got what they'd been longing for: a trip to the NBA Finals. Led by Reggie Miller and Jalen Rose, the Pacers were a team of veterans who could rebound, defend, and flat-out shoot the basketball. Eight Pacers players shot 36% or better from three-point range. And while Reggie averaged fewer points than in the past, he saved his best for when it really mattered.

In the 2000 NBA Finals, the Pacers faced Shaquille O' Neal, Kobe Bryant, and the Los Angeles Lakers. The ferocious duo was attempting to lead the Lakers to their first title since 1990. Many predicted that L.A.

would make quick work of Indiana. They were younger, stronger, faster, and more athletic. But the Pacers hadn't come this far to roll over for a new champion. At the age of 34, Reggie was past the point in his career where he could put up 24 points per game over the course of a whole season. But in the NBA Finals, Reggie upped his scoring and he and Jalen Rose combined to average 47 points per game.

The Pacers won Games 3 and 5 in Indiana, but they eventually fell to the Lakers in a hard-fought Game 6 in L.A. In Game 6, the Pacers led by five points going into the fourth quarter, but Shaquille O'Neal was simply too much to overcome. His 41 points and 12 rebounds led the Lakers to a narrow five-point

Breaking Through
After heartbreaking losses in the Eastern Conference Finals in 1998 and 1999, the Pacers made it all the way to the NBA Finals in 2000.

victory. Over the course of the series, Shaq had averaged 38 points and 17 rebounds in one of the most impressive Finals performances in NBA history.

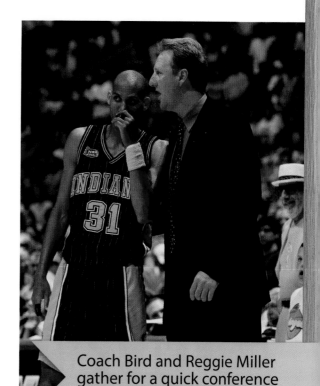

Coach Bird and Reggie Miller gather for a quick conference on the sidelines.

The final game of Reggie Miller's career was played on May 19th, 2005. In a loss to the NBA Champion Detroit Pistons, Reggie hit four threes and scored 27. The Pacers had endured a year filled with adversity. An incident with the Pistons earlier in the season had led to the suspension of a number of key players. But Reggie and his teammates never stopped trying. Reggie had given 18 years of service to the Pacers. He had led them to the playoffs 13 times, and played his best when the lights shone the brightest. Entering the 2005 playoffs, Reggie was determined to fight to the end. The Pacers surprised many by upsetting the Atlantic Division champion Boston Celtics in the first round. Facing the NBA Champion Pistons, Reggie's Pacers took a 2-1 series lead before succumbing to defeat.

In the years that followed Reggie's departure, the Pacers struggled to rebuild. They had lost

Reggie waves to the fans, following his final game at Conseco Fieldhouse.

Hall of Pacers

a Hall of Fame player and their emotional leader. Subsequently, Pacers fans pinned their hopes on a few players who let them down. The joy began to drain from the game they had loved so well.

Indiana basketball fans, above all, desire to see the game played the right way. Forget winning championships. Reggie never won one and he was beloved. Pacers fans expect the same of their professional team that they expect of their high school players. They want to see teams playing together, sacrificing for one another, and respecting the game. Once it was

Frank Vogel coaches the Pacers' new group of selfless standouts.

perceived that the Pacers had lost their way, that they not only played selfishly but without a spirit of joy, the fans' interest waned. It was up to hometown hero Larry Bird to rebuild a team that the city of Indianapolis and the state of Indiana would once again be proud to call their own. In the 2011-12 lockout-shortened season, the Pacers took a giant step in the right direction.

Coached by Frank Vogel and managed by Bird, the Pacers' core of humble standouts led the team to their best record since 2004. They beat out the Boston Celtics and the Atlanta Hawks to earn the #3 seed in the playoffs. Then they beat the Orlando Magic to earn their first

Danny Granger and David West celebrate a playoff victory against the Orlando Magic.

playoff series victory in seven years.

The Pacers entered the second round of the playoffs as underdogs to LeBron James, Dwyane Wade, and the Miami Heat. NBA analysts admitted that the Pacers were tough and could cause the Heat some problems. However, most of them couldn't imagine how

Roy Hibbert challenges a shot by Dwayne Wade.

a team without any superstars could compete with a team that had two of the league's top-five players. Those who counted the Pacers out hadn't been paying close enough attention to this squad. The team was deep. They

Terrifying Trio

All-Stars LeBron James and Chris Bosh joined All-Star Dwyane Wade in Miami in 2011.

rebounded extremely well, had one of the top ten defenses in the league, and in players like Danny Granger, David West, Roy Hibbert, George Hill, and Paul George they had scoring threats from every conceivable position on the floor. Also, much to the delight of Indiana basketball fans, this team played together. They were disciplined, unselfish, and gave their all every night. They played with the chemistry and joy that had been at the heart of Indiana's love affair with basketball for nearly a century. In 2012, they nearly shocked the world.

After losing a tight game in Miami to open the series, the Pacers trailed the Heat by five points at halftime of Game 2. Playing good defense but unable to get their shots to fall, the series appeared to be playing out as the analysts had predicted. Then the two teams came out of the locker rooms and the rest of the nation got to see why Pacers fever had returned to Indiana. The Pacers outscored the Heat 28-14 in the third quarter and held on down the stretch to win the game. As players began to celebrate the upset victory, veteran David West urged his team-mates to get off the floor. The message was clear: our work is not done. The Pacers were not content with advancing to the second round of the playoffs. They were not content with one upset victory over the Heat in Miami. Maybe analysts hadn't expected them to be playing in the Eastern Conference Semifinals, but they had expected it of themselves. Now they expected to win.

The Pacers came home for Game 3 to Bankers Life Fieldhouse, and 18,000 ecstatic fans rejoiced

Danny Granger rises over Mike Miller for a jump shot during Game 2 of the Eastern Conference Semifinals.

Larry's Legend Grows

In 2012, Larry Bird won Executive of the Year, becoming the first person in the history of the league to win MVP, Coach of the Year, and Executive of the Year.

as their squad destroyed the Heat. The game wasn't even close. Granger, West, and Hill all scored in double figures and Roy Hibbert had one of his best games of his career. The 7'4" center scored 19 points, grabbed 18 rebounds, and blocked five shots as the Pacers cruised to an easy victory. The 2012 Pacers were proving to be bigger and tougher than the mighty Heat. Unfortunately, the Heat still had a king, and in 2012, King James would not be denied his first NBA crown.

If the rest of this series made Pacers fans flash back to unpleasant memories of Shaquille O' Neal in 2000, it would be understandable.

Roy Hibbert shows his gratitude to the Pacers' fans as Game 3 draws to a close.

In Game 4 alone, LeBron James scored 40 points, grabbed 18 boards and dished out nine assists. He and Dwyane Wade, determined to win their first championship as teammates, took their game to another level. It was a level that the Pacers were unable to match. The once-soaring hopes of Indiana's players and fans came crashing back down to earth. The Pacers were an excellent team. They had improved dramatically and turned themselves into a real threat in the Eastern Conference. But they were not quite good enough to beat the eventual champs. Still, thrilled by their team's resurgence, fans eagerly awaited the start of the next season.

The 2012-13 season started with bad news. Expectations were higher than they'd been since Reggie Miller wore the Pacers' blue and gold, but an injury to star forward Danny Granger dampened those hopes. The Pacers struggled out of the gate to a 3-6 record but then they found their stride. By early January, swingman Paul George had earned his first trip to the NBA All-Star Game, and by the early April, the Pacers had beat out the Chicago Bulls to secure their first Central Division title since the 2003-04 season.

It's hard to say what lies in store for the Pacers and their fans. But the goal of finally winning an NBA crown has not changed. Reggie Miller may be gone but Donnie Walsh, the man who brought him to Indiana, has returned to the front office. The Pacers have expert management, an excellent coaching staff, and a number of dedicated stars that play the right way. They compete with the tenacity of an Indiana high school athlete, trying desperately to make the varsity squad. With that kind of work ethic, who's to say how far this team will go? It's no secret which teams the Pacers will have to go through in order to win the title. It's no secret that those teams have superstars. But it's also no secret that the Pacers have the talent to beat any of those superstars on a given night.

These Pacers would be well served to read about their heritage, to listen to the stories of the Milan Indians or Crispus Attucks High. History shows us that the state of Indiana is the mecca of the basketball world. The time has come for the Pacers to stand at the top of that world and make some history of their own.

Paul George leaps over teammates Roy Hibbert and Dahntay Jones during the 2012 NBA Slam Dunk Contest.